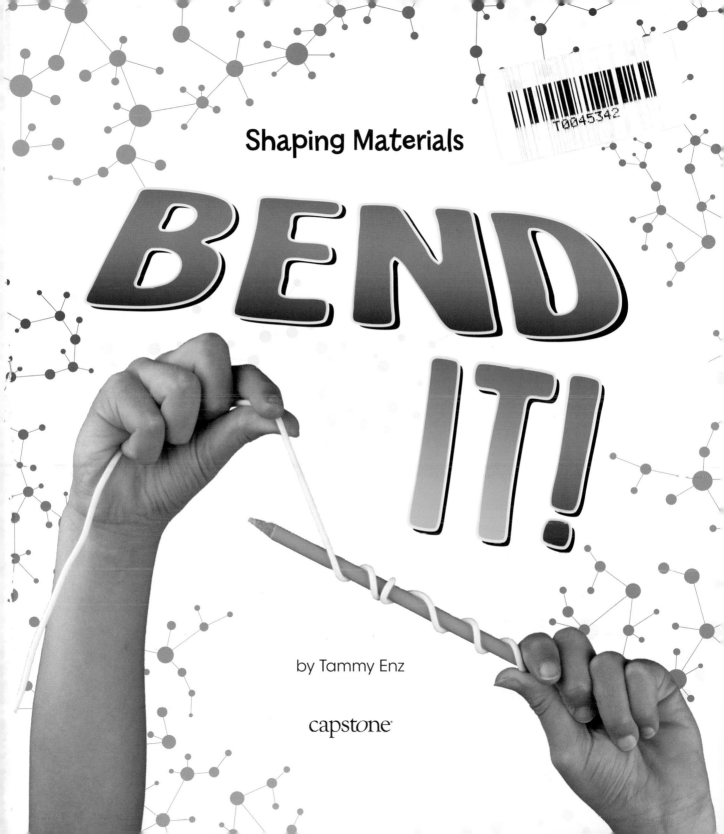

Shaping Materials

BEND IT!

by Tammy Enz

capstone

© 2018 Heinemann Raintree
an imprint of Capstone Global Library, LLC
Chicago, Illinois

To contact Capstone Global Library, please call 800-747-4992,
or visit our web site www.capstonepub.com

All rights reserved. No part of this publication may be reproduced or transmitted in any form or by
any means, electronic or mechanical, including photocopying, recording, taping, or any information
storage and retrieval system, without permission in writing from the publisher.

Edited by Linda Staniford
Designed by Kayla Rossow
Original illustrations © Capstone Global Library Limited 2018
Picture research by Kelli Lageson
Production by Victoria Fitzgerald
Originated by Capstone Global Library Ltd

21 20 19 18 17
10 9 8 7 6 5 4 3 2 1

Library of Congress Cataloging-in-Publication Data
Library of Congress Cataloging-in-Publication Data is available on the Library of Congress website.
ISBN: 978-1-4846-4097-5 (library hardcover)
ISBN: 978-1-4846-4101-9 (paperback)
ISBN: 978-1-4846-4105-7 (eBook PDF)

This book has been officially leveled using the F&P Text Level Gradient™ Leveling System.

Acknowledgments
We would like to thank the following for permission to reproduce photographs: Capstone Studio:
Karon Dubke, cover, back cover, 1, 5, 8, 9, 10, 12, 13, 14, 15, 18, 19, 22, (top left and bottom right);
Shutterstock: Hisae Aihara, 11, jack_photo, 6, McCarthy's PhotoWorks, 17, Natasha R. Graham,
cover (background), Olesia Bilkei, 4, photocritical, 20, 22, (middle right), pro500, throughout
(background), ruzanna, 21, Sebastian Nicolae, 7, 22, (top right); Thinkstock: eugenesergeev, 16, 22,
(bottom left)Every effort has been made to contact copyright holders of material reproduced in this
book. Any omissions will be rectified in subsequent printings if notice is given to the publisher.

All the Internet addresses (URLs) given in this book were valid at the time of going to press.
However, due to the dynamic nature of the Internet, some addresses may have changed, or sites
may have changed or ceased to exist since publication. While the author and publisher regret any
inconvenience this may cause readers, no responsibility for any such changes can be accepted by
either the author or the publisher.

Printed and bound in China
PO010438F17

Table of Contents

Some words are shown in bold, **like this**.
You can find out what they mean by looking
in the glossary.

What Bends?

When you **bend** a material,
you change its shape.
A bent object has a curve
or angle to it.

But what happens when you try to bend a pencil? Or a thick book? Some things bend and **spring** back. Other things break. Some don't bend at all.

Easy Benders

Try bending a wire paperclip. It bends **easily**. Things that bend easily are called **pliable**.

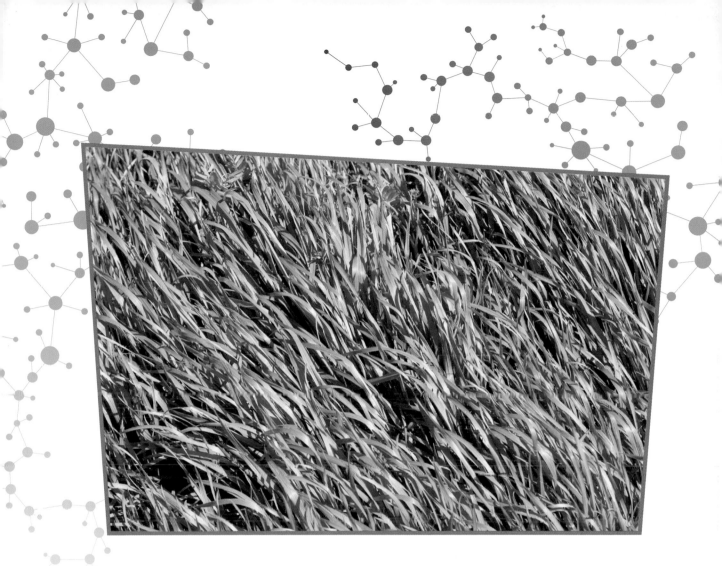

A cloth towel is pliable.
So are thin plastic, cardboard,
and paper objects. Soft pasta
is pliable. So is a blade of grass.

Project:
Paper Hat

Make this hat by folding pliable paper.

You Will Need:

- Rectangular piece of paper

What To Do:

1. Fold the paper in half.
2. Fold the corners from the crease into the center.
3. Bend up the bottom flaps.
4. Open your hat and wear it.
5. Notice how the folded paper keeps its new shape.

Materials That Spring Back

When you fold paper, it stays bent. But what happens if you don't fold it? It springs back!

Materials that spring back when bent are called **elastic**. Elastic things go back to their shape after bending. Try pulling a rubber band. It springs back. Bend a small twig. It springs back too.

Projec : Ca apul

Use a wooden craft stick to make this catapult.
Its spring action can fling candy.

You Will Need:

- 2 wooden craft sticks
- Rubber band
- Pencil cap eraser
- Small piece of candy

What To Do:
1. Stack the two sticks.
2. Wrap the rubber band tightly around both sticks at one end.
3. Wedge the eraser between the sticks.
4. Place the candy near the end of the raised stick.
5. Push down on the raised end of the stick.
6. Let go to fling the candy.
7. Notice how the stick bends but then snaps back into its original shape.

Materials That Break

If you bend some materials too far, they break. Things that break easily are called **brittle**. Glass is brittle. So is an eggshell.

Project: Puzzle Sandwiches

Try making these brittle sandwiches.

You Will Need:
- 4 graham crackers
- Icing or peanut butter

What To Do:

1. Bend and break each cracker into three or four pieces.
2. Find two pieces that are the same shape.
3. Stack them together with icing between.
4. Find other pieces that are the same to make more sandwiches.
5. Eat!
6. Notice how the crackers are brittle and snap easily when you bend them.

Changers

Brittle materials don't always stay brittle. Some can become **pliable**. Some materials change when heated. Others change when soaked in water. Pasta becomes pliable when put in hot water. If bent when wet, the pasta will stay bent when it dries.

Most metal is hard to bend.
But it becomes pliable when
heated. If metal is bent when hot,
it will stay bent when it cools.

Project:
Spaghetti Snakes

Make these snakes to see a material change from pliable to brittle.

You Will Need:

- 3–5 pieces of cooked spaghetti
- 2–3 pencils
- Waxed paper
- Optional: paint, googly eyes, glue

What To Do:
1. Wrap a piece of spaghetti around each pencil.
2. Lay the pencils on waxed paper to dry.
3. Bend other pieces into squiggles.
4. Lay on waxed paper.
5. Let the snakes dry overnight.
6. Optional: paint and glue on eyes when dry.
7. Notice how the spaghetti was pliable when it was wet, but is brittle now that it is dry.

You Bend It!

Try bending things you find around you. Find materials that don't bend.

Look for pliable, elastic, and brittle things. Ask an adult to help you find things that bend more easily when heated. Are there materials that bend better when wet?

Picture Glossary

bend   to make something curved or angled

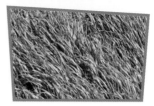

brittle   easy to snap or break

elastic   able to stretch out and return to its original size and shape

pliable   easy to bend

spring   to return to its original shape after being bent, stretched or pressed down

Find Out More

Foelker, Rita. *Origami Fun for Kids.*
New Clarendon, Vt.: Tuttle, 2016.

Laughlin, Kara. *Fun Things to do with Paper Cups and Plates.* 10 Things to Do. Mankato, Minn.: Capstone, 2014.

Marshall, Pam. *From Tree to Paper.*
Start to Finish. Minneapolis, Minn.: Lerner, 2013.

Riley, Peter. *Everyday Materials.* Ways Into Science. London, U.K.: Franklin Watts, 2014.

Use FactHound to find Internet sites related to this book.

Visit *www.facthound.com*

Just type in 9781484640975 and go!

Super-cool stuff!

Check out projects, games and lots more at
www.capstonekids.com

Index